Nature's Children

MONARCH BUTTERFLY

Bill Ivy

Grolier

FACTS IN BRIEF

Classification of the Monarch Butterfly
    Class: *Insecta* (insects)
    Order: *Lepidoptera* (butterflies)
    Family: *Danaidae* (milkweed butterfly family)
    Genus: *Danaus*
    Species: *Danaus plexippus*

World distribution.   North, South and Central America, Europe and Australia.

Habitat.   Requires warm sunny weather and access to the milkweed plant.

Distinctive physical characteristics.   Orange wings with black lines and a black border with rows of small white spots.

Habits.   Slow deliberate flight; active in daytime; eggs laid on milkweed plant; migrates in large swarms to southern United States, Mexico and Central America for the winter.

Diet.   Nectar of flowers, preferably milkweed blooms.

Published originally as
"Getting to Know . . . Nature's Children."

This series is approved and recommended by the Federation of Ontario Naturalists.

Canadian Cataloguing in Publication Data

Ivy, Bill, 1953-
  Monarch butterfly

(Getting to know—nature's children)
Includes index.
ISBN 0-7172-1923-2

1. Monarch butterfly—Juvenile literature.
I. Title.   II. Series.

QL561.D3I95 1985   j595.78'9   C85-098722-9

Contents

If you sit quietly by a flower garden on a summer afternoon you may be lucky enough to see a butterfly. It is probably looking in the flowers for food.

There are thousands of different kinds of butterflies in the world. Some are almost as big as dinner plates. Others have brilliant colors. Still others, such as the Swallowtail, even have long "tails."

Butterflies come in a wide variety of shapes, colors and sizes, but they all share one thing. They all go through four stages in their lives. You could say that people go through stages too. We all start life as babies, grow into children, then teenagers and finally adults. But through all of these stages we do not change all that much; we just get bigger.

A butterfly looks *very* different in each stage of its life. It starts out as a tiny egg and hatches into a many-legged caterpillar. Then this caterpillar curls up and is wrapped with a thin covering. When it finally breaks out of this "shell" it is a beautiful flying creature—a butterfly.

The Royal Butterfly

Most people agree that the lion is the King of Beasts. But do you know who is king of the butterfly world? It is the Monarch, of course, as its very name suggests.

And no wonder the Monarch Butterfly is considered the king of butterflies. Although their paper-thin wings are fragile and delicate, some Monarchs fly the length of North America twice in their short lifetimes.

And long-distance flying is just one chapter in the Monarch's amazing life story. Shall we follow it through the others?

The Monarch, like most butterflies, comes out during the day. A moth, on the other hand, comes out at night.

Milkweed Muncher

If you have milkweed plants near your house, you probably also have Monarch Butterflies. The Monarch depends on the milkweed for food and a place to lay its eggs.

Wherever the milkweed grows, the Monarch soon follows. Long ago, Monarch Butterflies were found only in North, South and Central America, but now they also live in Europe and Australia. No one knows how the Monarch managed to cross the oceans, but we do know that when the milkweed plant spread to new countries so too did the Monarch.

The Monarch mother is careful to lay only one egg per plant so that there will be plenty of food for each caterpillar to grow on.

Small Beginnings

The Monarch Butterfly begins its incredible life as a tiny ridged egg no bigger than the head of a pin. When the female butterfly is ready to lay her eggs she carefully searches for suitable milkweed plants. She seems to know that the caterpillars that will soon hatch from the eggs will need fresh, tender leaves to eat. So she is careful to choose only young, healthy plants.

The mother Monarch lays her eggs one by one on the underside of milkweed leaves. When she is done she will have laid about 400 eggs.

You would have to look very carefully to see a newly laid Monarch egg because its creamy yellow color blends in perfectly with the milkweed leaf. But as the caterpillar grows inside it, the egg changes color. It becomes yellow, then light gray and finally dark gray. Then the shiny black head of the newly formed caterpillar can be seen through the egg shell. Four days to a week after the Monarch egg is laid, the caterpillar chews a hole through the egg and slowly crawls out. A caterpillar is born!

Opposite page:

The Monarch mom carefully glues each egg to the underside of a milkweed leaf.

The Eating Machine

Although the newly hatched caterpillar, or "larva," is tiny—only two millimetres (less than one-eighth inch) long—it has an enormous appetite. After dining on its own eggshell, the caterpillar begins to eat the milkweed plant from under its own feet. This miniature eating machine feeds day and night, only briefly stopping to rest between meals. It can eat a whole milkweed leaf in only four minutes. It has very strong jaws and, unlike you, it chews sideways.

During the first day of its life the caterpillar eats its own weight in food. Soon it is twice as big as when it hatched. Yet its life is not one long, happy picnic. It can easily drown in a drop of water, and it has a difficult time protecting itself from hungry birds or other caterpillar-eaters.

Can you imagine eating your own weight in food in a single day? That's what this tiny new Monarch caterpillar is doing, and in about two weeks it will be the size of the full-grown caterpillar you see here with it.

Caterpillar Closeup

After two weeks of almost non-stop eating, the yellow, black and white Monarch caterpillar is about five centimetres (2 inches) long, and it weighs 2700 times more than when it hatched.

Its body is made up of thirteen ring-like sections. Instead of a nose, the caterpillar breathes through holes in these sections. These breathing holes, or "spiracles," look like the portholes along the side of a ship.

On the underside of the caterpillar's body are six small legs and five pairs of large claspers which the caterpillar uses to grip with. It is hard to believe that this worm-like creature will one day become a graceful butterfly.

Yellow, black and white bands make this Monarch caterpillar easy to spot.

Heads or Tails?

You might have trouble telling the caterpillar's head from its tail. Both have long black feelers growing out of them. But if you looked closely you would see that one set of feelers was longer than the other. The longer feelers are on the caterpillar's head.

These head feelers are called "antennae," and the caterpillar uses them to feel its way around. That is important because, although the caterpillar   very small and its e

Which end is which—can you tell?

Talented Tail

Having a tail that looks like a head is useful to the caterpillar. It confuses birds and other animals that like to eat caterpillars, just as it confused you. To avoid being eaten, the caterpillar wiggles its tail at predators. This protects the caterpillar's head by drawing attention to its tail, where a bite will cause less damage. If that does not work, the Monarch caterpillar may drop off its milkweed plant onto the ground. There it will play dead until the danger has passed. Then the caterpillar will often climb back onto the same milkweed.

The caterpillar's tail feelers are also useful to swish away pesky flies that try to lay their eggs on its back.

The Monarch caterpillar often hangs upside down while enjoying a tasty meal of milkweed.

Preparing for Change

When they are fully grown, Monarch caterpillars eat voraciously. They are preparing for an amazing series of changes that will transform them from slow-moving caterpillars to brightly colored, darting butterflies.

The first signal of the changes to come is that they become very restless. Some leave the milkweed plants that have been their homes since hatching. They wander for as long as two days, looking for a safe place to undergo their amazing transformation. Most choose a spot high off the ground so that they are out of the reach of hungry field mice or other insect-eaters.

Once it has found a safe spot, the caterpillar uses a special gland in its mouth to weave a small silk button underneath a twig or leaf. Turning around, the caterpillar hooks its rear claspers into the silk. Then it swings free, to hang upside down in the shape of the letter "J." What will happen next?

The Little Green House

The caterpillar begins to move. First it arches its back, forcing the skin to split open. Then it wriggles for up to five hours to shed its coat for the last time. When its old skin is gone it looks like a large green water droplet. It has entered its pupa stage.

Slowly this thick, green drop begins to change shape and color. Its outer layer hardens into an elegant emerald case, decorated with gold. This is known as a chrysalis, which comes from the Greek word for golden. The Monarch's little green house with the single ring of golden dots around it hangs perfectly still, but inside something amazing is happening.

This Monarch caterpillar shed its skin four times while it was growing. Now it is shedding for the fifth and final time. It is ending its life as a caterpillar and entering the pupa stage.

Monarch Magic

Inside the chrysalis one of the great wonders of life is taking place. No one fully understands just how this miraculous change happens, but from the soft green liquid inside the chrysalis an adult butterfly will be formed.

For the next nine to fifteen days all is still. Then almost magically, the chrysalis shell turns a rich teal blue and gradually becomes totally transparent. The adult monarch is now visible, its miniature flame-colored wings and jet black body cramped inside. Hanging head down it waits for the right moment to break out of its jeweled cage.

It's hard to believe that inside these two "little green houses" caterpillars are getting ready to become butterflies.

A Brand New Butterfly

The Monarch Butterfly instinctively knows just the right moment to emerge from the chrysalis. It will not come out on a rainy or cool day because it must be warm to be active.

Usually the Monarch emerges on a bright sunny morning. The colorful case stirs and a tiny slit appears on the bottom of it. The chrysalis continues to rip open, and within two minutes a rumpled form tumbles out in a backward somersault and clings to the empty chrysalis.

A butterfly is born!

Taking Wing

The new butterfly has limp, crumpled wings that look like folded parachutes. Immediately, they begin to unfold as the butterfly pumps them full of body fluid from its swollen body. It takes 20 minutes before its wings are full size.

Slowly the Monarch begins to sway back and forth and joins the two halves of its tongue together to form a tube. This is very important for it is this tube that enables it to eat. Next the Monarch rests, waiting for the warmth of the sun to dry and harden its wings. Then, for the first time in its life, this royal butterfly rises up on delicate wings and flies.

It takes about one hour for the butterfly's wings to harden. Until that happens, the butterfly cannot fly.

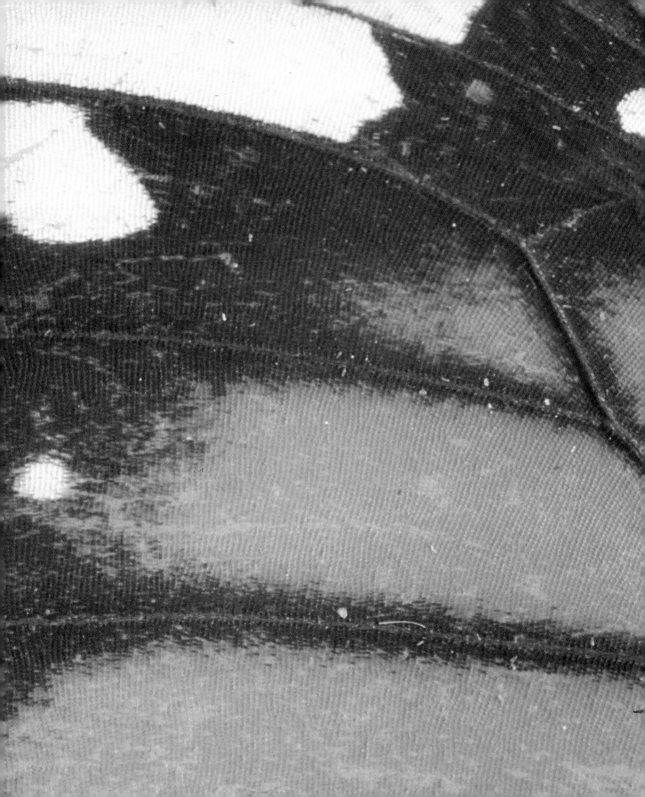

Meet the Monarch

The Monarch has two pairs of vividly patterned wings, covered with millions of tiny, colored scales. These overlap each other like shingles on a roof.

If you were to touch the Monarch's wings these dainty flakes would rub off like fine powder onto your fingers. This is why the family name for butterflies and their relatives, the moths, is "Lepidoptera," a Greek word meaning scale-winged.

Like all insects, the Monarch has six legs and three body sections: the head, thorax and abdomen. But for some reason this butterfly does not seem to need all its six legs. It always holds the front pair folded up close to its body.

The bright colors on the wings are really layers of scales. Underneath the scales the wings themselves are transparent.

Monarch Senses

It is hard to imagine using the soles of your feet for tasting foods but that is what a Monarch does. And a Monarch's feet are much more sensitive to sweetness than your tongue is.

Stranger still are the Monarch's bulging eyes. They seem much too big for its head. It is no wonder they are so big; each large eye contains 6000 lenses! No one is sure how the world looks to a Monarch, but we know that it can detect movement better than almost any other living creature. Just try to catch one!

Despite its superb eyesight, this surprising butterfly relies even more on its sense of smell. Two antennae attached to its head act as the Monarch's nose and ears. They are very sensitive and help direct the Monarch to its favorite flowers.

This Monarch, like most butterflies, has knobs on the ends of its antennae.

Flower Food

In less than a month the Monarch has gone through four stages of life: egg, caterpillar, pupa and adult butterfly. No more changes will take place, nor will the Monarch Butterfly grow. But even though it has stopped growing it still needs energy, so it must eat.

For its first three days as a butterfly the Monarch feeds constantly. Instead of eating leaves as it did as a caterpillar it lives on the nectar of flowers—the same sweet fluid bees use to make honey. The Monarch flits from flower to flower using its hollow tongue to drink the nectar which has formed in the blossom of the flower. When not in use, this handy built-in straw is coiled under the butterfly's head.

Stamp, stamp, yum. Like all butterflies, the Monarch tastes with its feet.

A Happy Wanderer

After feasting for three days, the Monarch butterfly drifts aimlessly over fields and meadows. It may travel great distances in its wanderings, sleeping in any handy tree or bush at night, pausing at any handy flower for a meal when it gets hungry.

Although the Monarch needs the warmth of the sun and loves bright sunny weather, it is often seen flying just before a thunderstorm. For this reason it has been nicknamed the storm butterfly.

When the milkweed is in bloom, Monarchs will choose its flowers over all others. But if there are none around, any flower will do just fine.

Predators Beware!

The Monarch can fly out of the way of ground-dwelling predators such as shrews and mice, and it has come up with an unusual way of defending itself against fast-flying birds. It has a bitter taste that can be poisonous to a bird if it swallows too much butterfly. The Monarch tastes this way because of chemicals in the milkweed plant which it ate as a caterpillar. Birds soon learn that orange and black butterflies are not good food and avoid them.

Another kind of butterfly, the Viceroy, makes good use of the Monarch's bird-proof taste. It looks so much like a Monarch that birds leave it alone as well, even though they would probably find the Viceroy a tasty snack. The Viceroy's Monarch "disguise" is a very effective way of protecting it from hungry birds.

Even though they are look-alikes, there is one way to tell a Viceroy butterfly from a Monarch butterfly. Look at their hind wings. The Viceroy has a black line across its hind wings that the Monarch does not have.

Incredible Journey

Monarchs are the only insects that fly south for the winter. They start out alone as soon as the winds of autumn turn cold, but they may gather in large groups as they wait for good conditions at difficult crossing points. Then they sometimes continue on their long voyage together. Many will travel almost 3200 kilometres (2000 miles) before they reach their final destination. These migrating swarms can become very large, sometimes numbering in the millions.

The red leaves of autumn tell us this Monarch will soon be gone.

The Monarchs travel by day at about the same speed as a fast jogger, occasionally stopping to feed. Just one "tankful" of nectar can keep them going for a week or more. With good winds pushing them some have been known to travel 130 kilometres (80 miles) in a single day.

The Monarchs follow the same routes and land in the same trees that generations of Monarchs have before them. That is amazing because many of these butterflies have never made the trip before. How they do this is one of the mysteries of the astonishing Monarch.

Winter in the South

Try to imagine so many Monarch Butterflies that you cannot see the bark of the trees that they are roosting on. You cannot see any leaves or pine needles either—just Monarchs, Monarchs, everywhere! Some of these "butterfly trees" become so heavily laden with Monarchs that their branches may actually snap under the weight!

Monarchs from western North America congregate in California along the Pacific coast. Monarchs from eastern North America head for Mexico. One of the most famous of the Monarch's winter "resorts" is Pacific Grove, California. Each year the school children in that area hold a parade to celebrate the Monarchs' arrival.

All winter long, the Monarchs rarely leave their "butterfly trees" except to feed. With the arrival of spring, they are ready to wing their way northward again.

Northward Bound

Many of the Monarchs mate before leaving their winter resting place or on the journey home. They do not stay together after they mate. Instead alone or in small groups they slowly head north. Along the way some of the females stop to lay their eggs. In four to six weeks these eggs will hatch into caterpillars and be transformed into butterflies. By instinct the new butterflies know that they must continue north. And by instinct they know when they have reached their summer homes.

Not all of the butterflies that start the journey finish it. Few Monarchs live to be four years old, and many die on the long hard flights. But there are always new butterflies hatching to take their place in the great northward migration.

Words to Know

Caterpillar   The second stage in a Monarch's life. Also called the *larva*.

Chrysalis   The hard case that covers the pupa.

Claspers   The grasping hooks that a caterpillar uses to hold onto a leaf.

Gland   A part of the body where certain substances are made.

Larva   The caterpillar stage of a butterfly or moth's life.

Lens   One part of an insect's eye which helps it to see objects.

Life cycle   The stages in an animal's life from birth to death.

Mate   To come together to produce young.

Migration   A journey that many animals and the Monarch Butterfly make in search of food.

Molting   Shedding old skin or feathers to make way for new.

Nectar   The sweet liquid produced by plants which some insects drink.

Pupa   The stage in a butterfly or moth's life before it turns into an adult.

INDEX

Cover Photo: K. Janosi (Valan Photos)
Photo Credits: Bill Ivy, pages 4, 8, 11, 12, 18, 19, 20, 22, 24, 27, 29, 30, 33, 37, 39, 41, 42; Norman Lightfoot (Eco-Art Productions), pages 7, 14; Herman H. Giethoorn (Valan Photos), page 34; T.W. Hall (Parks Canada), page 45.